Homecoming
by Microlight

Homecoming by Microlight

Landscapes and Satires

DAVID MORPHET

First published in 2015 by

Notion Books
11 Daisy Lane
London
SW6 3DD
www.notionbooks.co.uk

Copyright © David Morphet 2015

The right of David Morphet to be identified as the author of this work has been asserted by him in accordance with the Copyright, Designs and Patents Act 1988

All rights reserved. No part of this book may be reproduced, stored in a retrieval system, or transmitted, in any form or by any means, without the prior permission in writing of the author. Requests to publish work from this book should be made to Notion Books.

ISBN 978-0-9575458-2-3

Design by Helen Swansbourne

By the same author:

Poetry

Seventy-Seven Poems
The Angel and the Fox
Approaching Animals from A to Z
39 Ways of Looking
The Silence of Green
The Maze – a daydream in five cantos
The Intruders
Lyrics from the Periodic Table
A Sequence from the Cyclades
Night Train to Utopia
Satires and Legacies

Biography

Louis Jennings MP,
Editor of the *New York Times* and Tory Democrat

The following have appeared in earlier collections by David Morphet: *Moorland (Seventy-Seven Poems); Ley Lines; Chapel-le-Dale; Swallow-holes (The Angel and the Fox); Pen-y-Ghent; Winter day above Dent; Intrusion (39 Ways of Looking); Song of Wool; Moor Song (The Silence of Green); Whatever; Return to the Pennines (The Intruders). Part of a trial run was published in The Eagle (2011).*

I am like a tree,
From my top boughs I can see
The footprints that led up to me.

> R S THOMAS (1913–2000)
> from *Here (Tares)* (1961)

Difficile est saturam non scribere.
It is difficult *not* to write satire.

> JUVENAL (*c.* 55 – *c.* 140 AD)
> *Satires* Book 1, line 30

Contents

Landscapes

Homecoming by Microlight	12
Song of wool	15
Colne Valley 1949	16
A vision of *Mallard*	17
Ley lines	18
Chapel-le-Dale	20
Selside, Settle, Bell Busk, Kettlewell	21
Swallow-holes	22
White nights at Dent	24
Winter day above Dent	25
Resurrection at Dent	27
Moor Song	28
Moorland	29
Here is no manifesto	31
Generous margins	32
Moorings	33
Moor cloud and mist	34
Moor mines	35
Intrusion	36
Ode to the *Settle and Carlisle*	38
Pen-y-Ghent	40
Return to the Pennines	41

Satires

Fox reappears	44
Residual value	46
Part of a trial run	48
No safety net	49
Turning the page	50
Seven questions	51
Whatever	52
Trading up	53
You have to hope the judge will sort things out	55
The reason why	56
The house that Jack bought	57
Eight untraditional nursery rhymes	58
A trip with Sybil Tours	61
Steel-capped PR	62
i) Meeting *Fayke*	
ii) The *Sons of Albion*	
iii) A *Steel-capped* proposition ...	
iv) ... which is turned down ...	
v) ... with consequences ...	
vi) ... and a troubling residue	
Out of sight	71

Landscapes

Homecoming by Microlight

Dreaming, I give myself a day to travel back
North, to all my native Pennine places –
boyhood in the valley of the Colne
between loud mills and silent moors,
and onward to the Dales –
one day to cover all that valued ground!

I fix to make my way by Microlight –
getting the truest take from up above –
and start by circling where the Colne
draws first life from the moorland cloughs
among a scattering of farms and cottages –
the moor's-edge parish of my mother's kin.

I say the names of all those cottages
and who was born there as I skim above
the rough pasture and the dark grey byres
and the church for which my granddad dressed the
   stone;
and think of my boy-delight at the great belch of
   smoke
as heavy goods trains plunged here deep
               into Standedge tunnel's gaping throat.

As I fly low over yards and alleyways
                           of close-packed villages,
decades decompress. A lane, a spire, a school
revive the flows and manifolds
that prospered my beginnings.

Through memory's binoculars I spy, again and
   again,
heart-held figures in familiar places.

Then on I navigate to cobbled Dent
by way of Settle, Selside, Ribblehead,
where my father's father saw the light of day.
I overfly the nose of Pen-y-Ghent
and follow the hard-won moorland railway line,
winding in thin air over long-limbed viaducts.

I swing past Ingleborough's potholed flanks
and, nodding down to the church in Chapel-le-Dale,
scatter sheep as I round the valley head
towards High Birkwith where the by-road stalls;
then up Cam Beck and over to Halton Gill
to follow Skirwith's flow down Littondale.

Everywhere there's stone – stone chimney-stacks,
stone mills, stone terraces, stone farms,
field upon field squared off by dry stone walls,
escarpment stone in frozen cataracts,
dark Millstone Grit, grey Horton Flags,
white limestone pavements cracked with clint and
   gryke:

littered, bare, erratic, boulder stones;
ascetic stone in windswept hillside Zions;
stone in upland graveyards and the heights
which three unquiet sisters made their own;
stone in Rawthey's fluid madrigal;
stone in the broad-flagged crevices of Dee

And above all the subtly-shaded moors
stretch out as far as eye can see,
sun glinting off the tarns and reservoirs.
So long as fuel lasts I'll fly
from Bleaklow up to Mallerstang and back.
Only mist and rain can make me stop.

Song of wool

River water, swift and soft,
rising up in valley mist,
swelling thread of warp and weft.

Elemental wool. Its smell
stoppering nostrils, rank and full,
carcassed in a canvas bale.

Tireless metronome of loom.
Hammering and deafening crash
of steel-tipped shuttle slamming home.

Young boy on a blackened floor
watching as the broad cloth grows,
listening as the steam-clouds pour

out hissing to the cobbled yard
where he'll linger with the fine
rusting things that mills discard.

Colne Valley 1949

The valley's my domain. I have the run of it.
My freedom's here and all my secret places –

long-worked-out quarries overgrown with gorse;
ruined mill-yards; sheds where no one comes.

Some days I count the trucks of coal-trains straining
at the valley's up-hill gradient, belching steam;

or I'll stick a farthing to the line with tar
and find, when the train's gone by, a flattened wren.

In spring I'll trawl for frogspawn in the derelict canal
and heave at the stubborn beams of abandoned locks.

I wade into the river blue with dye,
slipping on pebbles daubed with mill-waste slime.

I make a cave within the crevices
of bales of raw wool piled on warehouse floors.

I watch as men climb slowly, rung by rung,
spider ladders clamped to towering stacks.

Valley time is set by valley mills.
I know when their sirens wail it's time for home.

Coal burns in every house in every street.
Running back, I taste the acrid smoke.

A vision of *Mallard*

Side by side here there's the wool-dyed Colne,
a moribund canal and, rising above all,
the hard-worked line to Lancashire,
with gritstone ramparts holding back
the hillside like a castle wall.

All through the valley you can hear
the slow trundle and the up-line pant
of goods trains with a quarter mile of coal.
On windless days you'll catch, from the valley head,
the distant clatter of a down express.

Hour after hour beside the track I watch
the straining, slow, prosaic *Austerities*,
dreaming that *Mallard* will one day veer away
from its mainline flight and sweep up through our hills,
painting the valley with a flash of blue.

Ley Lines

Dent Town and Horton, Ingleton,
triangulate the high dales
where roots run deep.

The Dee, the Doe, the Ribble,
and their becks and viaducts
draw lines on the mind's map.

Lea Yeat and Gearstones,
Whernside, Hewthwaite, Rash,
mark out old memories.

At Chapel-le-Dale, St Leonard's,
squat and robust,
like the first churches of the North,

is holding ground
for Christ and in its element –
stone-hewn, an omphalos.

The Cam Beck tumbles down
past flags of Nether Lodge
into the swirl of Ribble.

The Dee ducks in and out
of thirsty strata, longing
for the Rawthey and the Lune.

This is the country of resilience,
big in its moorland boots,
and on its own two feet.

Chapel-le-Dale

A little child, I helped my stiff-legged grandpa
feed his chickens nearly sixty years ago;
and sixty years before, a little boy,
he also tagged along behind the pails
in this porous dale of cracks and caves and fissures,
where the streams duck underground
and moors scale Whernside;
mount up Ingleborough.

This is the hill; and this the well
where he watered the horses. Here is the gate
into the rough pasture; nothing much has changed.
Here are my grandpa's cousins, lying hard
beside the lych-gate wall; and here
the valley chapel holds its ground –
its roots sunk deep down in a close-cropped land
of limestone clint and tonsured scar.

Here, the memorials; here, the tale
of railwaymen who died round Ribblehead,
pushing the line through moorland to Carlisle.
I see my grandpa as a boy
made to sit upright in his Sunday pew
in the narrow nave, and wonder
who now remembers him but I,
or knows of his beginning here, and his belonging.

Selside, Settle, Bell Busk, Kettlewell

The aunt who told me can no longer tell
tales of what she gathered long ago
of Selside, Settle, Bell Busk, Kettlewell.

Adrift by Colne, she felt the spell
of never-fading names; her Avalon
was Selside, Settle, Bell Busk, Kettlewell.

And for her sake I won't forget the shell
which, for her, echoed myth and memory –
Selside, Settle, Bell Busk, Kettlewell.

Swallow-holes

Our maps define the limestone dale we're in,
and also show us what's beneath the skin
of field and fell. Among the contour lines
are pockmark swallow-holes, like ancient mines.

These are the avens plunging to deep veins
in the rock's fracture; splintered souterrains
spreading across an obscure hinterland.
Unseen, dark rivers flow there; lakes expand.

A world apart, the bowelled aquifers;
the dripping caverns with their long fingers
of lime; the buried waters trickling by
without disturbance; no observing eye

to detect them in their slow processes –
contaminate – pierce their unconsciousness.
Deep below ground, the hidden measures serve
to hold, accumulate, keep in reserve.

And yet the upper landscape answers
to their capacities; the river dries or dances
according to their appetite; it swells
when they are swollen; and when they thirst, it fails.

Explorers I salute; those who descend
and penetrate, and push on to the end,
exhausted, always hoping that beyond a
last dark channel they will find a wonder.

The wonder, though, remains in what's unseen;
the narrow capillaries; the whole machine
with its elaborate vessels, filters
of mineral, rich with minute particulars.

The wonder lies in courses of a deep
and hidden purity, the constant seep
of waters, and in due time their issuing
into a flight of streams, a sudden spring.

White nights at Dent

Each summer, years ago, we pitched our tent
in an open field in the sunken dale
under fells which funnel the road to Dent.

Dent, with the stream that ducks and weaves
under and over its limestone bed –
a water that beckons and deceives.

Dent, with its scattering of farms
held in diagrams of stone
four-square against the Pennine storms.

And in our white pavilion all night long
we'd hear the bleat of shed lambs from the fold
and ewes distressed and calling for their young.

Winter day above Dent

High in this circle of familiar hills,
mind fuses with their stretch and rising,
moulds to their wrap and folding,
and the sweep of scar and gill;

and down where Helm's Knott swells,
stubbled with heather, latches on
to the great Fault splitting Lakes from Dales,
where Pennines butt up against Lakeland fell.

All unity, the valley's scoop appears
from this vantage-point, but underground
the strata are at odds: one step and you're out
by a hundred million years.

Swift becks lay bare the skeleton;
disclose the fractures and the shattered bones
of breccia and conglomerate –
the twist and grind and shudder of convulsion.

But in the dale, a daub of green and brown
covers the sync- and anti-cline.
Its soft contours mantle the rend and fission
which aeons of wind and rain have whittled down.

Now all is calm. The fossil shells
and coral colonies lie silent
under upland farms. Deep seams of limestone
bed down quietly with shale.

Sedge glows in the setting winter sun
like fox's fur: long capes of shadow fall
from dry-stone walls: ice underfoot
warns that the short bright day will soon be done.

Resurrection at Dent

In rain-swept Dent, the day of resurrection
won't look like Stanley Spencer's sunny Cookham.
No bright Thames Valley light will shine on heaving
    graves.
There'll be nothing in the setting to suggest
a nice reviving cup of tea

and maybe a regatta on the river
once everything's been straightened out
and the tombstones put back neatly.
No sense of a brass band standing by
to play Jerusalem, or the Old Hundredth.

In Dent, it will be sombre and reserved.
The weather will be Pennine, with a mist
descending on the churchyard, its memorials
shrouded as the farming dead arise.
Sheep will move through everything like ghosts.

Pouring rain will put the damper on
triumphal choruses of hallelujah
or uplifting recitals of the Beatitudes.
The most you might expect to hear will be
a muttering of shorter psalms.

At a given signal, the whole band, mud on their feet,
will file down to the flatlands by the river
and, crossing the local Jordan in good order,
toil up the steep flanks of the dale to heaven,
hailing kin in dialect, or Norse.

Moor Song

Here is my element.
The lift and swell
and lip and lie.
The stretch of sky
over the hills.
The way moor folds;
the way it breaks
into a run of ghylls;
the way it falls;
the way the wide fells
hold the eye and all
is clear and still.

Moorland

The moor has a dialect
abrupt and guttural,
harsh and impoverished.

It is the sharp tongue of the wind
berating the bracken;
and the yatter of rain.

It is the hawk's cry
and the hare's scream,
and the low cough of grouse.

Swarthy the moor's complexion;
its skin of peat
pocked with reed colonies,

and heather primed
for autumn's explosion
into purple erysipelas.

It partners the sky.
The two of them cohabit,
blend and intersect.

The morning mist
brings a confinement
of all horizons;

while the wester sun
burns its image
on the moorland pools.

This unhedged margin
is our borderland
and needful wilderness.

May its rough thirst
never be slaked by fertile lime,
or by the dew of pasture.

Here is no manifesto

Maybe I'm up to the shins
in squelch and bog
but what is here
is sane and curative.

Moor curtains off
all power-sound –
all stridency and screech
and clangour and cacophony.

Here is no manifesto
to set teeth on edge.
No raucous canvassing.
No loud agenda.

Moor is inward
and impersonal
and passive
and remote –

an empty tract
under an open sky.
Transparent, calm,
unamplified.

Generous margins

Season after season I return
to the moor's wide-open book,
its generous margins,
its untrimmed pages,
the passages I've learned by heart.

Whatever time of year, I never tire
of the boldness of its print,
its breadth of coverage –
taut syllables of autumn ling,
dark punctuations in the snow.

Moorings

Grit and limestone outcrops
anchor my oldest moorings.

My thought-path follows a moorland spine
in every season.

Come thick cloud and louring mist
it knows to keep the contour of the fells.

Come crosswind and blinding rain
it knows to drop below the valley-heads

and follow the gills to sheltering stone.

Moor cloud and mist

There's low cloud, and a curtain falls,
shrouding and dousing shape and colour,
vision withered to a frieze of grey,
horizon shrunk down to a fringe of heather.

I know the moor in every season, every weather,
even blizzard, even driving snow,
finding my way down hard-ice gullies
to frozen reservoirs below.

Part of me wants always to be where
low cloud is closing in on ling
and, beyond cattle-gate and grid,
a cloak of mist is falling.

Moor mines

They knew their job, the tunicked engineers
who stripped out tin from Cornwall, gold from Wales,
and northward took a shine to Pennine lead,
shipping off smelted pigs with Caesar's stamp
to plumb the pipes and baths of Rome.

For centuries the search went on
for lustre of galena till the moors
were riddled with a slew of worked-out pits
and mile after mile of darkened galleries.
Slides of rubble in ravines were left as no-one's legacy.

Now all that broad economy has gone –
the miners in their hundreds underground,
the haulers up, the washers out, the placers of
    explosives,
the pumpers and the sorters and the smelters.
What's left is grist for archaeologists –

half-ruined adits to abandoned mines,
scabs of gangue and toxic residue
where shanks of heather will not grow,
sterile skin on gill and scar,
carbuncles on the moor's flank.

Intrusion

High up the scarp, just
under the lid of cloud,
a pair of humdrum
railway carriages
are puttering smugly
past the flanks of Whernside
and of Pen-y-Ghent.

Rail has long had moorland's
measure, laying down laws
of tilt and gradient,
slicing through shaw and fell,
piercing pike and crag,
striding valley heads
on viaduct stilts.

Roads are milder – turn
and dip and tolerate
moor's encroachment.
When the right time comes,
the land won't hesitate
to take them back, quilt them
with reed and sphagnum.

But rail is bedded in
and with a deeper brand;
pick and dynamite have
scarred and cauterised.
Its track – even when green,
with the steel long gone –
will last like Pyramids.

Ode to the *Settle and Carlisle*

i)

There's nothing TGV about the *Settle and Carlisle*.
No super-speed. No *Shinkansen*.
No platform stretching half a mile.

It's not a line for those impressed
by the bustle of great termini.
The glory's in the durability –

the deep-sunk staples of its viaducts,
its ligature of bog and moss,
the fabric of the moor transfixed.

ii)

Stiff they stand, those long-shanked viaducts
braced hard against the Pennine gales

gaunt and bedded down to rock
through treacheries of swamp and clay,

making straight the way to Settle,
bringing Settle to Carlisle.

iii)

Tough little stations, squat and obstinate;
slate roofs steep-pitched to see off snow and ice;
well-found stores and well-banked fires
to see them through the winter's worst.

Unconquered outposts on the line's
audacious drive through watershed,
austere, robust and resolute.
Garsdale, Dent and Ribblehead.

Pen-y-Ghent

So to the nab of Pen-y-Ghent
where moor's impounded in a maze of walls
and landscape speaks in accents that I know –
a tongue of scars and rakes and becks
straight from the Norse. A land of spur and knoll,

rough pasture on the valley side,
a cold wind scouring over scarp
from Ribblehead. Here is my own;
my latitude and dialect,
my discourse and parole.

From this bleak Sinai the moors roll out
austere and puritan and fall
in tussock, stone and reed
sodden to the valley floors
down gill and swallow-hole.

If there's illusion here,
it's deeply rooted in the bone
and ineradicable.
This is native heath and home,
meridian and pole.

Return to the Pennines

Dusk brings me to my native hills
where limestone skeleton breaks through
a sodden moorland skin.

I watch long flanks of shadow darken
what's already drab and dark. I walk
where mosses huddle in deep fissures.

It's not geology that's brought me back,
or fossils, or an itch to hear
pebbles clatter down swallow-holes.

Nor am I after rushes or cotton-grass.
I'm not moved by a collector's urge
to fill botanic jars with specimens.

And I haven't come for the sake of listening to
the grate and clang of Viking names,
the kelds and thwaites and riggs and gills.

I've come because the sprawling Pennine script
is written deep inside me, and
in truth I read it every single day,

knowing the moorland trails by heart,
knowing my hands were meant from birth
to raise well-stacked cairns and strong drystone walls.

Satires

Fox reappears

I glimpse him passing in the terminal
as he struts from limousine to First Class Lounge.
It's Fox! I haven't heard of him in years.

He looks immensely smart and prosperous –
a Loden coat; designer shoes;
under his arm a case of supple leather.

I hail him with a warm *Well met!*
You do remember me of course!

With a quick glance at his watch he shows
he's little time to spare for Auld Acquaintance,
not least for a shabby one like me –
drab jacket; trousers bagging at the knee.

Oh yes, he says, *you were the ditherer*
who wouldn't listen to my good advice.
I do remember all too well
your constant 'on the one hand, on the other'.
What have you done in life? Stayed still?

Oh no, I say, *I muse a lot, and write.*
There's much to think about
and much to witness.
From time to time I launch a boat
on poetry's broad river.
He pulls a face and scoffs *And is that all?*
You should have been more ready to take risks,
more prompt to take your chances.

*Yours-Truly is a mover and a shaker.
I haven't waited on events.
I've made things happen!*

Like what? I ask him – and I know he'll bluff:
I've never heard him tell an honest story.
A bit of this, he says, *a bit of that.
I have a well-developed sense
of fruit that's ripe for plucking.*

As if the last word has been said,
he stalks off to the First Class Lounge
leaving a cloying scent of sham and musk.

Residual value

I'm glad to see the back of Fox
and tell myself that worldliness like that's
not made to last. But then I ask –

what's left of my own sparse balance-sheet?
From the outskirts of insolvency
I scan the entries. All are out of date.

* * *

Aged twenty-three, for law unqualified,
in an overhang of Empire I was made
a magistrate encharged with homicide.

Then I served the people's princes in their courts
and watched the cardinals and jesters strut
to reach the sun. They failed as like as not.

I joined the vanguard of a vocal band
of troubled folk all passionate to find
means to heal disturbance of the mind.

And for many years I made great play
with fissile megawatts and buckled rails
but scenes have long changed and casts slipped away.

* * *

Residual value? Those that I love – and verse –
I trust will be my relicts and I guess
the tally could be seriously worse.

Part of a trial run

Mirrors state quite flatly that I'm solid.
But reflection tells me that's a shallow view
which only on the face of things seems valid.

The fact is that I'm liquid to the core –
a sort of sponge infused with chemicals –
a saturated, vascular affair

of fluids right down to the bone.
Blood laced with iron. Salt in sweat and tears.
All kinds of compounds dribbling through my brain.

Genome swags festooned with chemo-codes
entwining and dispensing and enjoining,
launch infinitesimal cellular episodes –

atoms flickering in non-stop motion –
a constant switching through minute potentials –
instanteous bondings and dispersions –

all part of evolution's trial run
where inputs, imperceptibly adjusted,
are tested time and time again

to outcomes not infallibly predicted.

No safety net

Take tightrope walkers inching across a chasm –
even risking a dance-step over the drop –
or flying trapeze artists twisting and turning
yet somehow always catching the bar,
or rock climbers scaling an overhang
clinging to cracks by their fingertips –
they know what they're doing, don't they?
One slip, one unrecoverable step?
Shouldn't they have a safety net?
Well, that's for *them* to say.

As for desperate refugees
on the brink of free-fall –
a final tipping-point –
a short step from the edge –
(hopelessly unbalanced,
those countless uninsurables) –
what wouldn't *they* give for a safety net!

Turning the page

It's high time that we turned the page
booms the black-browed prophet –
*high time indeed to scrap the whole damned book
and shape up to the coming desert age
where a wild wind's blowing.*

No need, my friends, to turn the page
says the smooth-tongued politician.
*We're far from being at that stage.
This is a spring-like, plenteous age.
Fine crops are growing.*

What idiots want to turn the page?
growls the hedge-fund trader.
*This is the High Net Earner Age.
Accumulation's all the rage
and cash is flowing.*

I know just how to turn the page
says the tax consultant,
*raising my fees at every stage.
This truly is a Golden Age
and easy going.*

Seven questions

What is the point of disclosure, asked the politician,
when one question just leads to another?

What is the point of meetings, asked the chairman,
unless you have the Board under your thumb?

What is the point of a creed, cried the zealot,
without the power to enforce it?

What is the point of a uniform, asked the man who wore it,
unless you can push people around?

What is the point of facts, asked the lawyer,
except to floor your opponent?

What is the point of words, asked the author,
unless you can get them into print?

What is the point of anything, asked the banker,
unless you can turn it into hard cash?

Whatever

Asked if they thought that Heavy Metal turns
the brain to palpitating pulp from which
its neurons never perfectly recover,
they grabbed their i-Pods, muttering
Whatever.

Asked if they thought that truth is absolute,
or whether all attempts to prove it so
are nothing but an ethical manoeuvre,
they turned the volume up, and mouthed:
Whatever.

Asked if they knew that space is never-ending
and that our planet, if it lasts that long,
will end up in a fiery supernova,
they tuned to R & B and mocked:
Whatever.

Asked if they reckoned death was terminal
or karma's ticket to reincarnation
where soul will prove, in some shape, a survivor,
they switched to hip-hop, rapping out:
What-ev-er.

Asked finally if all seemed for the good
or if they thought the skies were growing dark
and the wise thing was to head for cover,
they put on funk full blast and snarled:
What. Ever.

Trading up

He started off with little more
than a modest Trust and an Old School Tie
and the rentals from a mansion block.
No one guessed he'd aim so high.
But all his life he traded up.

He traded up against the Trust
He traded up against the block.
All he ever did was trade
until his fortune had been made
from bricks and mortar, this and that.

He bought his stables, bought his yacht.
He bought an island in the sun.
He bought a title and a gong.
And when a good thing came along
he made sure that he bought the lot.

He bought advice to dodge his tax.
He bought an organ of the press.
He bought a two-mile wide estate,
surrounded by electric wire.
He posted guards. He posted dogs.

Of everything he bought the best –
his limousine, his private jet,
his art, his furniture, his wine,
his friends, his mistresses, his wives.
All this he did though trading up.

But then (he had no choice) he found
his heart and lungs were trading down,
his liver was in deficit,
he had a shortfall in the brain
and, babbling about trading up

and bidding low and selling high
and numbered bank accounts in Basle
and megabucks and bottom lines
and squeezing assets till they're dry
in hope of super-gains, he died.

You have to hope the judge will sort things out

Yes, yes – truth gets confused and knocked about
in courtrooms when the lawyers say their say.
You have to hope the judge will sort things out.

No telling fact's too small for them to scout
with parody that makes a stronger play
till truth gets all confused and knocked about.

Claiming the benefit of flimsy doubt
the nastiest of crooks can get away.
You have to hope the judge will sort things out.

Silky Counsel know well as they spout
that justice comes in many shades of grey
once truth has been confused and knocked about.

Decent, honest, truthful, fair ... devout?
What makes you think that these will win the day?
You have to hope the judge will sort things out.

Courts are rings where every single bout
sees blows below the belt. They're *cabarets*
where truth gets all confused and knocked about.
You have to hope the judge will sort things out.

The reason why

We know we have your order to fulfil
but the marketing director's gone home ill
and the head of distribution's at the shrink.

We know you have a query on the bill
but the departmental manager's gone AWOL
and the invoicing computer's on the blink.

We know the set-up leaflet isn't brill
but the copywriter lives in Guayaquil
and the printer in Hong Kong is low on ink.

We know the gadget's got a missing grill
but our agency mechanic lost the drill
and the anti-clockwise screw slipped down the sink.

We know the cistern is inclined to spill
but the ball-cock sub-contractor's gone downhill
and the cut-off valve supplier took to drink.

We know the freezer's apt to over-chill
but our quality control's in over-kill
and pushes each appliance to the brink.

We know the boiler sometimes doesn't fill
and the timer fails to operate, but still ...
the weather's mild.
                        Which gives us time to think.

The house that Jack bought

This is the house that Jack bought.

This is the mortgage that funded the house that Jack bought.

This is the bank that sold the mortgage that funded the house that Jack bought.

This is the debt that sunk the bank that sold the mortgage that funded the house that Jack bought.

This is the tax that paid the debt and saved the bank that sold the mortgage that funded the house that Jack bought.

This is Jack who paid the tax that paid the debt and saved the bank that sold the mortgage that funded the house that Jack bought.

Eight untraditional nursery rhymes

Rock a bye baby
on a tree top,
soon you shall have a Kalashnikov.
Cradle it in your arms so small
and down will come
mummy, daddy and all.

* * *

Mary's little lamb grew fat
and bold and unappealing.
It liked to ram her in the back.
Its smell would send her reeling.
The cherishing had gone too far.
She took it to the abattoir.

* * *

Sing a song of shooting-up
until you're on a high,
gabbling about blackbirds
baked in a pie.
When the pie is opened
you'll hear the blackbirds sing
while men in white coats come along
to take you in.

* * *

Boys in blue,
come blow on your horns.
The place has been pilfered,
the guard's been suborned.
But who's going to call them?
No, not I.
For if I do ...
... I may get fitted up.

* * *

I have a little Trust Fund
which keeps me from the cold.
It fills my boots with silver.
It fills my socks with gold.
Bankrupt barons' daughters
come to visit me
and all for the sake ...
of my irresistible charm.

* * *

I saw a ship a-sailing,
a-sailing on the sea
and O it all was laden
with stricken refugees.
There was no sign of captain
or crew upon the deck.
They'd left the ship a-drifting
They'd left the ship to wreck.

* * *

Diddle diddle dumpling
my son John
is a proper little neocon.
He goes to bed with his gun strapped on
and dreams of bombing everyone.
Diddle diddle dumpling
Bomb! Bomb! Bomb!

* * *

Hey diddle diddle,
fat cats on the fiddle
and non-doms over the moon.
The launderers laughed to see such fun
and the bankers ran off with the spoons.

A trip with Sybil Tours

With ever-enterprising Sybil Tours,
we took an *End-of-Season Special* trip
to *Night-spots of the Elysian Fields*.

Virgil, our driver, said he'd been before,
but seemed a bit uneasy with it all.
Back of the bus, the singing nuns, he said,
were putting him off, and half the front
were high on angel dust.

On the ferry, fares had rocketed
and no one could understand the ferryman
who kept on muttering about
the cost of dying.

We rolled in after dark. A minder asked
the older trippers what they made of it.
Too quiet, they replied. *It's much too quiet.*
We thought we'd come to see
Illuminations.

An old man added, panting, bleary-eyed,
Yes – and some real Celebrities.
Not just that crowd
of half-starved extras wearing long white shirts
all standing round as if the show is over.

Steel-capped PR

i) Meeting *Fayke*

From the muddle in my bedside drawer
a crumpled ticket tumbles out.
Uncertain what the ticket's for

I hold it closer to the light
and find my eye drawn to a gap
where panelling has come apart.

I press. A click. A door slides back
to show a spacious entrance hall,
a *Welcome* plaque, a moving stair

rising with a gentle hum,
soft music in the atmosphere.
A voice intones *So glad you've come!*

I'm swept up on the moving stair
to an atrium of chrome and glass
and step off on a marble floor

beside an electronic screen
with an urgent cursor racing on
repeatedly in red and green.

A swoosh of red proclaims a class
on *How to place the blame;* then green
zips by with *How to sell the pass!!* –

with exclamation marks in red.
Then – green again – a seminar
on *Engineering disrepute*.

It seems I've reached the fountain-head
of a firm called *Snarlings*. On the wall
an ice-blue neon logo reads:

*World-leaders in **Steel-capped PR**.*
A suave man with a sun-bronzed face
appears. Silk jacket. Well-groomed hair.

Hello-o he cries. *So glad you've come!*
He smirks and damply shakes my hand.
To my surprise he knows my name.

He has some spiel he wants to spill
and clears his throat and starts to boast
of *things that have been handled well*.

Hold on, I stutter. *Not so fast!*
I've only just stepped off that stair.
I've no idea who you are.

The suave man frowns. *My name is Fayke –*
that's F-A-Y- ...I'm CEO
of Snarlings, famous for bespoke

PR solutions. Mark my word –
our firm is at the cutting edge –
we go where angels fear to tread.

Which sounds a step too far... I say
*I can't think why you're glad I've come.
I'm unimpassioned by PR.*

You'll soon find out he says *but first
please listen. Snarlings lead the world.
Our business model is the best!*

*It's thirty years and more since Snarlings
pioneered **Steel-capped PR**.
That's when the firm first made a killing*

*out of mockery and gibe.
While others peddled puff and hype
we carved a niche in diatribe,*

*sensing long-pent-up demand
from people who were keen to strike
but anxious to conceal their hand.*

*Our clientele just grew and grew
once they saw what we can do
to pull to pieces and pursue*

*with our corps of **Steel-capped** personnel
chosen with the utmost care
for skill wherever business calls –*

*that's politics, finance and law,
commerce, medicine, academe,
religion, journalism, war.*

*For every job we seek the cream
of those with records of distortion,
fabrication, swindling, scheming,*

*travesty, disinformation.
innuendo, slur and gloss,
I have to say we're spoiled for choice.*

*Unfrocked, struck off, cashiered, disbarred –
feathered in every false pretence –
the wild geese flap in by the score.*

*Newsmen are our sharpest blade.
The vanguard are a hard-nosed team
from the rough end of the tabloid trade.*

ii) The *Sons of Albion*

Stop! I cry. *You've got me wrong.
I've heard enough. It's not my scene.
That's not a pack where I belong.*

He pauses. *We've been taken on
for a vastly lucrative campaign
by a Group I do not care to name*

*though I'll tell you they are large and strong
and their pockets are immensely deep.
Let's call them Sons of Albion.*

Their aims – I won't be too precise –
are radical and bellicose.
They wish to propagate with force

the creed that markets left alone
to work their own benign devices
are the country's vital cornerstone.

Key to that they wish to trash
all market rules and regulation
as unremitting balderdash.

They want an end to immigration,
welfare payments, human rights
and what they call 'insane taxation'.

They're burning with determination
to 'bring to heel' all those – they claim –
who've undermined the British Nation.

We're specially required to deal
remorselessly with Europhiles.
Top dollar when we make them squeal!

What a contract! What a steal!
What a field for taunt and scorn
and doctored anecdotes well-soled

with hobnails from our island story!
The fees! I can't wait to begin!
*It's **Steel-capped PR's** hour of glory!*

iii) A **Steel-capped** proposition ...

And where, you ask, do you come in?
Well, not for taunt or jibe or scorn.
We're well equipped for slur and spin.

But we lack a practised writer's ear –
a skilful word-smith who can spot
an inadvertent textual flaw

or plagiaristic lapse which might
expose the project to a sneer
or snide antagonistic slight.

For pots who call the kettle black
raw ridicule's the greatest fear.
It's vital we protect our back.

And that is what we want you for –
to warn us of banana skins
and keep all sniggers from the door.

Your mouth will water at the pay –
a bonus when the job goes right
and a crisp retainer every day.

Your own fine hand would never show.
You'd work in ultra-privacy.
I'd be the only one to know.

Nor would we ask you to adhere
to the project's aims, in whole or part –
the contract makes this crystal clear.

The scheme could last a year or more.
The hours are short. The work is light.
Your bank account would soar and soar.

The offer's nothing if not fair.
I trust you'll give it careful thought.
There is no trick – it's pure PR.

iv) ... which is turned down ...

I dithered. Could I bear to yield
to *Snarlings*' lucrative embrace
and let my standards slip, for gold?

Yet all I had to do to please
the authors of this Far-Right farce,
was dot the i's and cross the t's.

I wasn't asked to turn my coat.
My input would be undisclosed.
The work would leave me free to write.

A sow's ear rather than a purse?
I squirmed at queer **Steel-capped PR**.
But all that money? Could be worse?

I needed time and took a day
to balance out the pros and cons
then answered with a downright NO!.

v) ... with consequences ...

I thought I'd seen the end of it –
all traces of the episode
would fade away. But not a bit!

I found the story had been spread
that my pen – well-primed – would ply for hire.
My reputation was in shreds.

Worse, it was said my greed had grown
so much I'd got the market wrong
and turned a golden offer down.

The press jeered that they'd checked me out
*with sources privy to the facts
and whom they had no cause to doubt.*

I went to *Snarlings* in a huff.
The Fayke man bluffed *It wasn't us!
I guess the clients set you up.*

*Your 'No-no' made them most upset.
They thought we'd got you on the hook.
They see you as a renegade.*

<u>We</u> *said 'no comment' to the press
when they asked us if the tale was true.
We're sad of course it's come to this.*

So much for *Snarlings'* avatar
with his vow to keep me out of sight.
So much for vile ***Steel-capped PR.***

I can't see how to put things right.
My mood is bordering despair.
I'm shivering. I'm drenched in sweat ...

vi) ... and a troubling residue

And drenched in sweat I truly am
when, shaking, I wake up to find
with huge relief I'm in my room

and that there's been no smear, no sting.
The whole foul business was a dream
though the Fayke-man's neck I'd gladly wring

with all of his **Steel-capped PR's**
unfrocked, struck-off, cashiered, disbarred
black-propaganda privateers.

Can I now leave and close the door
for good on what was only dream?
Wipe the board clean? Or is there more?

I sense a stain, a scab, a scar,
a troubling real-life residue,
a feeling that there may be more;

that not by night but by light of day
some sour entanglement may come
that cannot be dissolved in dream –

that **Steel-capped's** never far away...

Out of sight

Alone in towns, he couldn't find,
of all the many doors,
one that was right.

Adrift, he spoke to passers-by
who took one sideways look and hurried off.
There was no kindness in the street.

He searched in skips for this and that.
He thought discarded magazines
might tell him things that he'd forgot.

He'd linger hours by public offices
until policemen moved him on,
sometimes gently; sometimes not.

Believe me. People often stopped to say
he should be found – they weren't sure how –
some place of refuge or retreat

where, calmed, he might conveniently stay
quite safe, quite still,
and out of sight.